FIVE
FINGER
PIANO
5

THE BEATLES HITS

T0085344

ISBN 978-1-4803-9307-3

HAL•LEONARD®
CORPORATION
7777 W. BLUEMOUND RD. P.O. BOX 13819 MILWAUKEE, WI 53213

Visit Hal Leonard Online at
www.halleonard.com

Eleanor Rigby

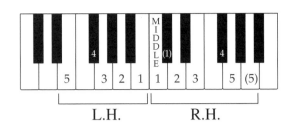

L.H.   R.H.

Words and Music by John Lennon
and Paul McCartney

Moderately, with a steady beat

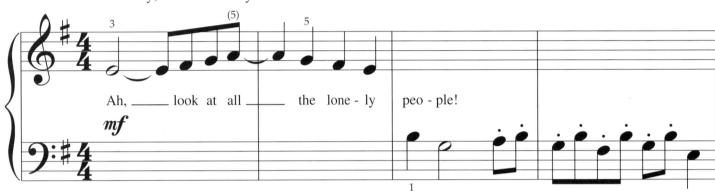

Ah, ____ look at all ____ the lone - ly peo - ple!

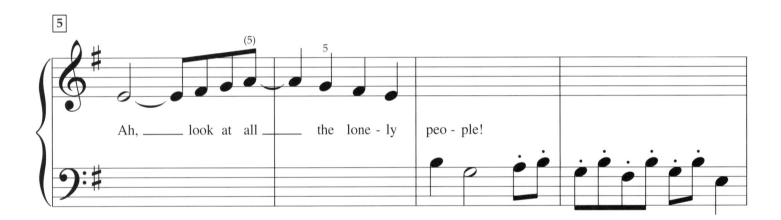

Ah, ____ look at all ____ the lone - ly peo - ple!

Duet Part (Student plays one octave higher than written.)

Moderately, with a steady beat

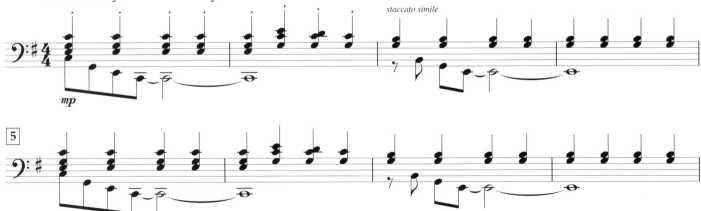

staccato simile

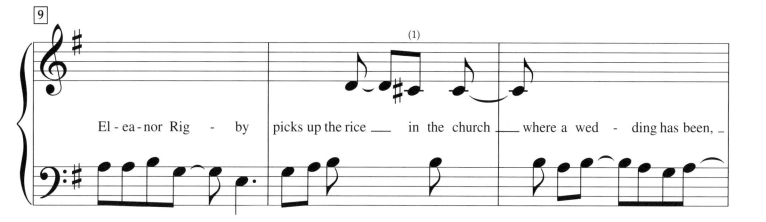

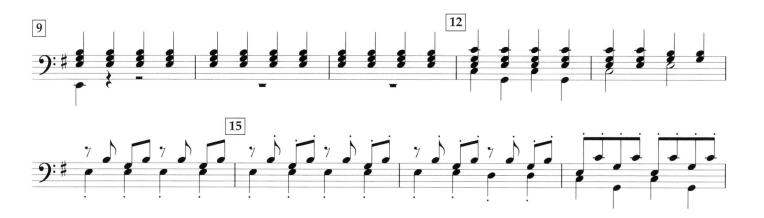

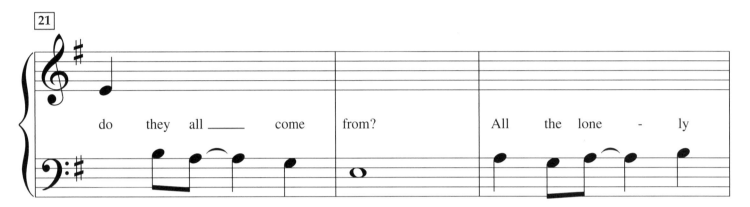

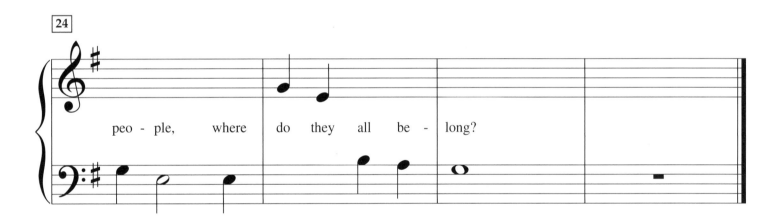

The Fool on the Hill

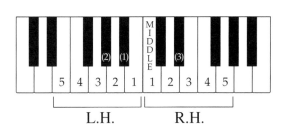

L.H.   R.H.

Words and Music by John Lennon
and Paul McCartney

Moderately

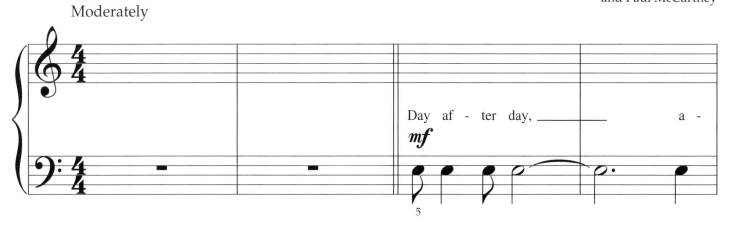

Day af - ter day, _____ a -

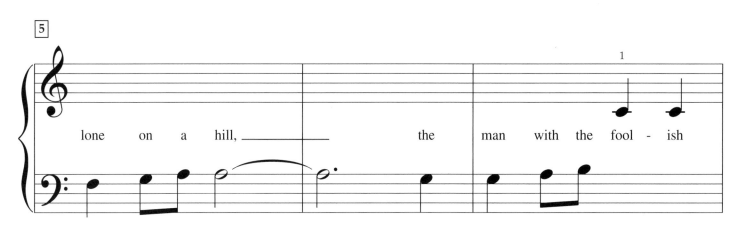

lone on a hill, _____ the man with the fool - ish

Duet Part (Student plays one octave higher than written.)

Moderately

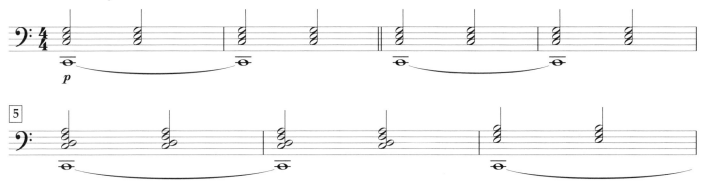

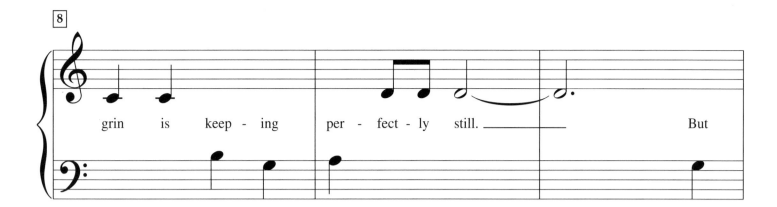

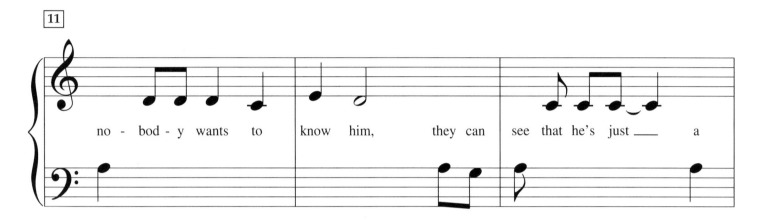

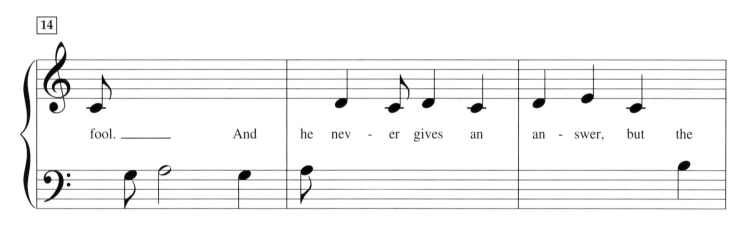

6

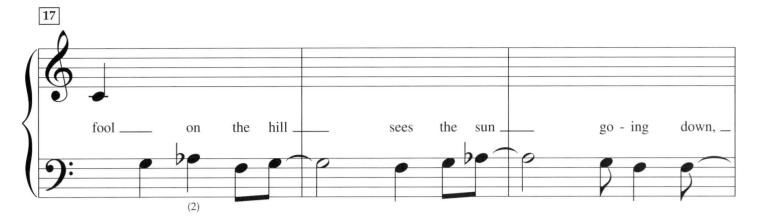

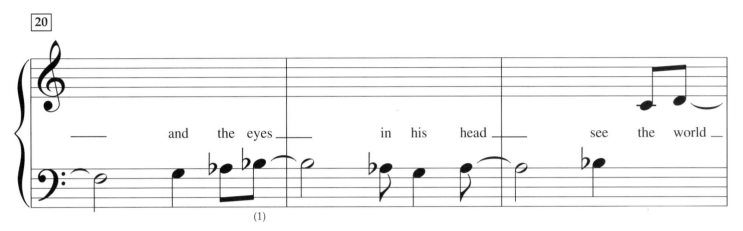

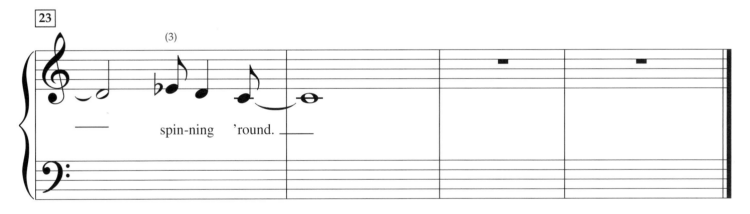

I Will

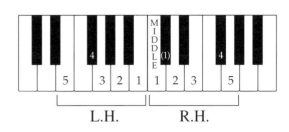

Words and Music by John Lennon
and Paul McCartney

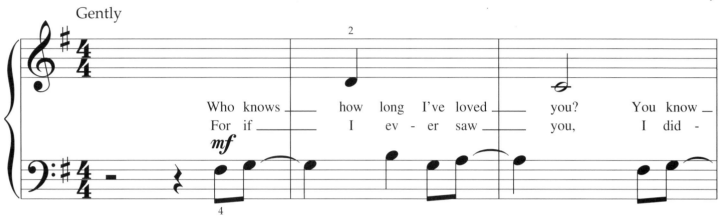

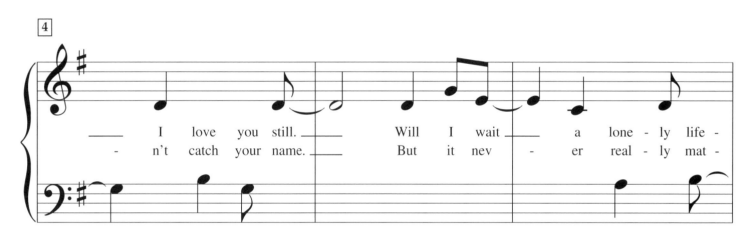

Duet Part (Student plays one octave higher than written.)

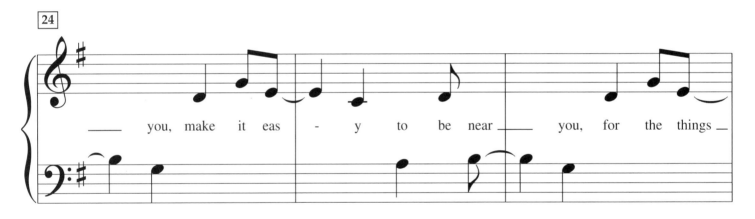

you do en-dear ___ you to me. Ah, you know ___ I will. ___

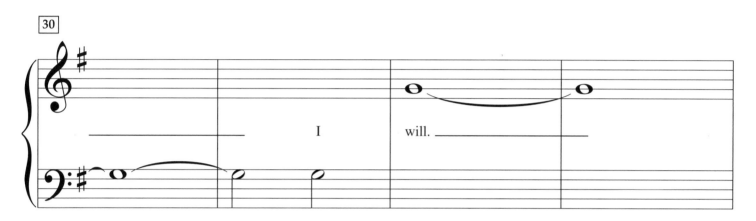

I will. ___

The Long and Winding Road

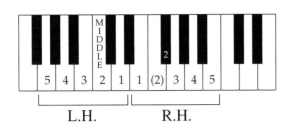

Words and Music by John Lennon
and Paul McCartney

Slowly

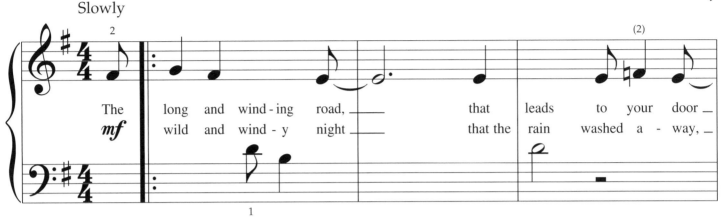

The long and wind-ing road, _____ that leads to your door _____
wild and wind-y night _____ that the rain washed a - way, _____

_____ will nev-er dis-ap-pear. I've seen that road be-
_____ has left a pool of tears cry-ing for the

Duet Part (Student plays one octave higher than written.)

Slowly

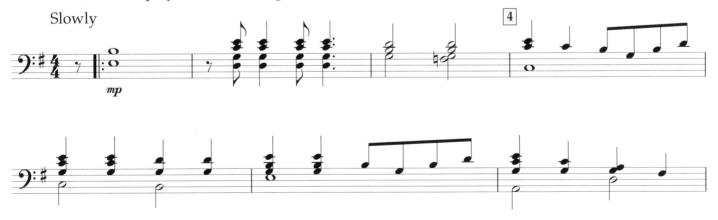

fore. _____ It al-ways leads me here. Lead me to your
day. _____ Why leave me stand - ing here? Let me know the

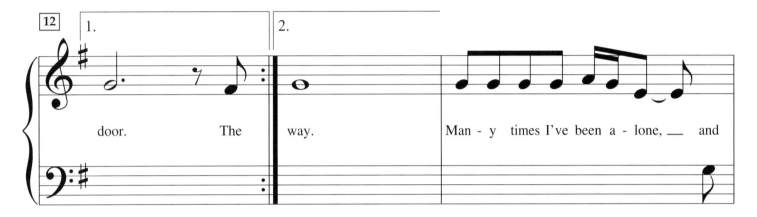

1. door. The way. **2.** Man - y times I've been a - lone, __ and

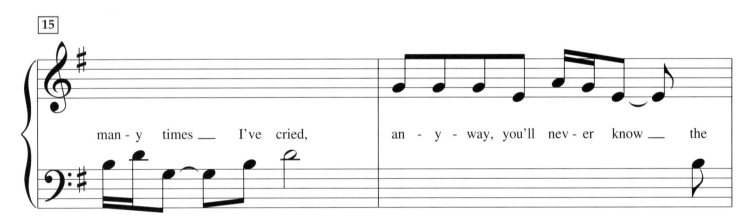

man - y times __ I've cried, an - y - way, you'll nev - er know __ the

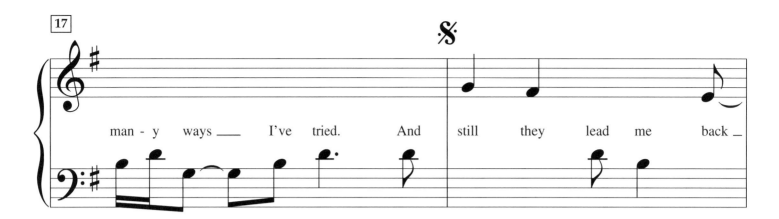

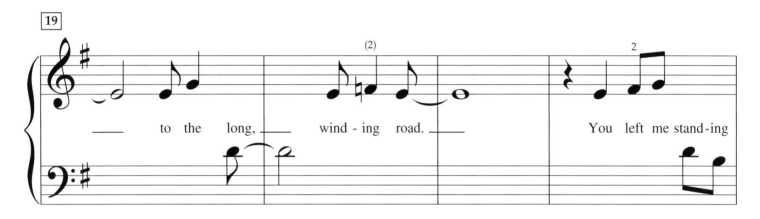

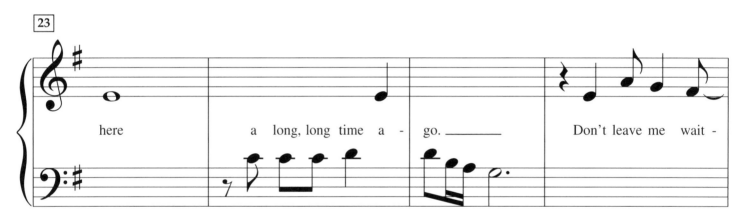

14

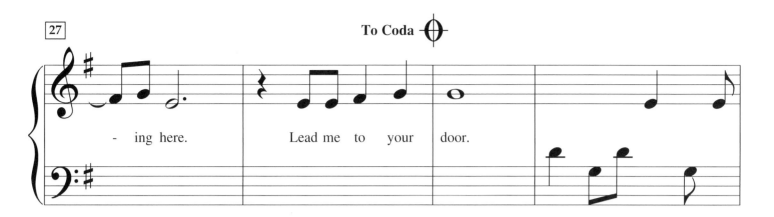

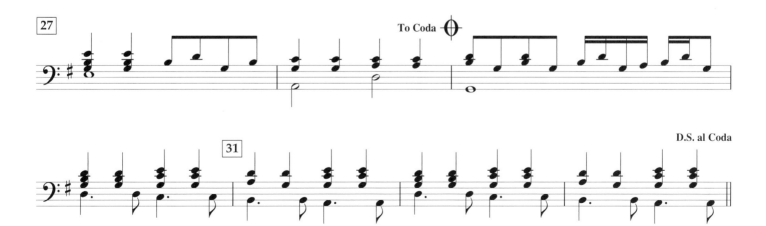

Love Me Do

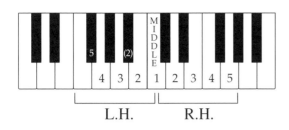

Words and Music by John Lennon
and Paul McCartney

Duet Part (Student plays one octave higher than written.)

Love, love me do, you know I love you. I'll

al - ways be true, so please _____

love me do. _____ Whoa _ love me do.

1.

(2)

17

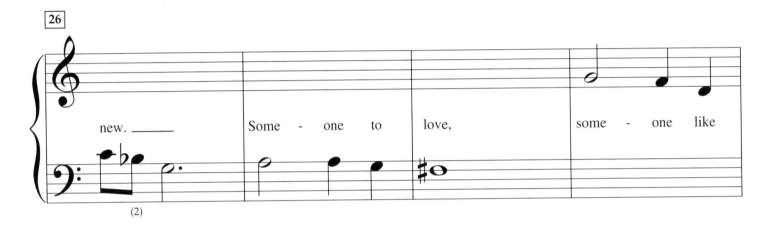

Nowhere Man

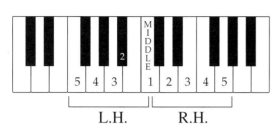

Words and Music by John Lennon
and Paul McCartney

Moderately

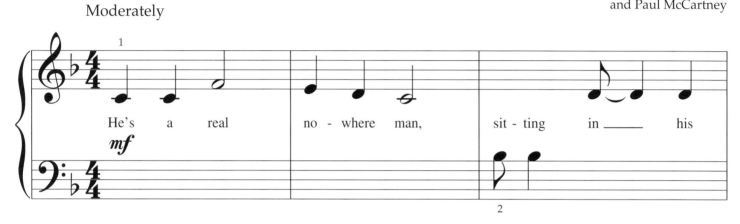

He's a real no - where man, sit - ting in ____ his

no - where land, mak - ing all ____ his no - where plans for

Duet Part (Student plays one octave higher than written.)

Moderately

20

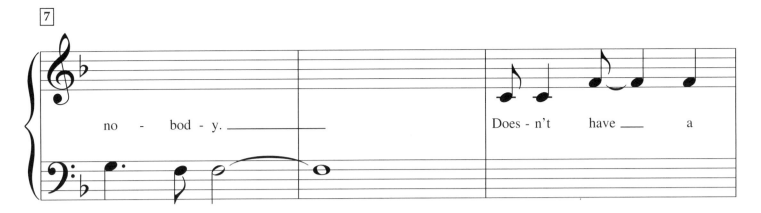

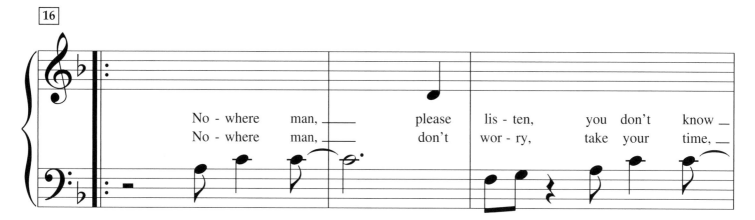

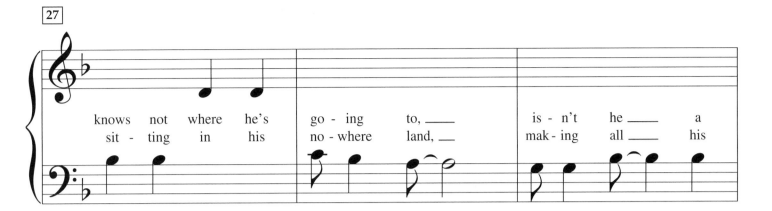

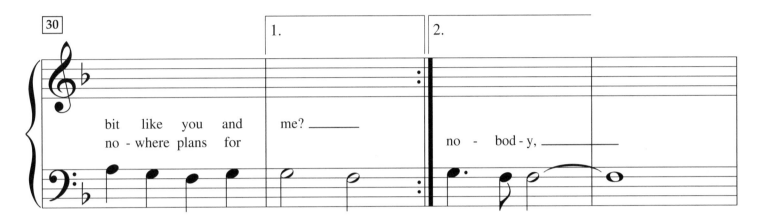

Penny Lane

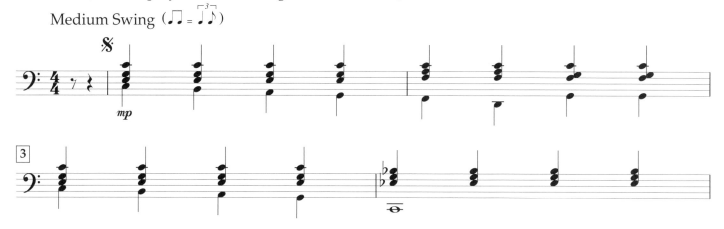

Words and Music by John Lennon
and Paul McCartney

Medium Swing

Lyrics (verse 1 / verse 2):

In Pen - ny Lane there is a bar - ber show - ing pho - to - graphs ___ of ev - 'ry
shel - ter in the mid - dle of the round - a - bout, ___ the pret - ty

head he's had the pleas - ure to ___ know. And all the
nurse is sell - ing pop - pies from a tray. And though she

Duet Part (Student plays one octave higher than written.)

Medium Swing

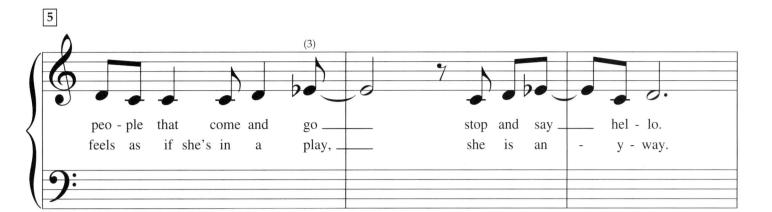

peo - ple that come and go _____ stop and say _____ hel - lo.
feels as if she's in a play, _____ she is an - y - way.

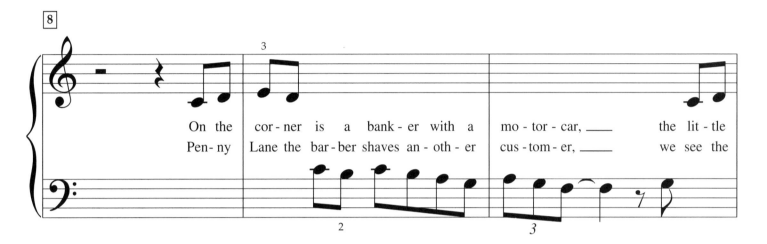

On the cor - ner is a bank - er with a mo - tor - car, _____ the lit - tle
Pen - ny Lane the bar - ber shaves an - oth - er cus - tom - er, _____ we see the

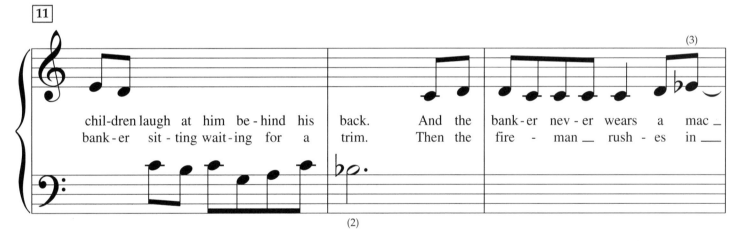

chil - dren laugh at him be - hind his back. And the bank - er nev - er wears a mac _____
bank - er sit - ting wait - ing for a trim. Then the fire - man _____ rush - es in _____

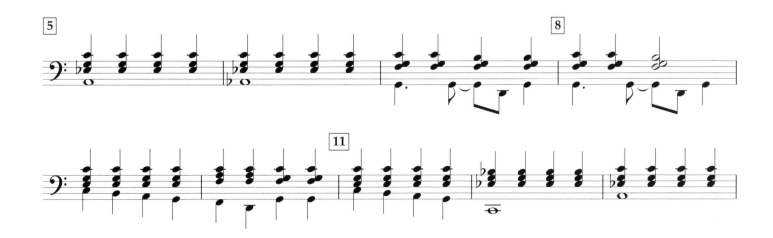

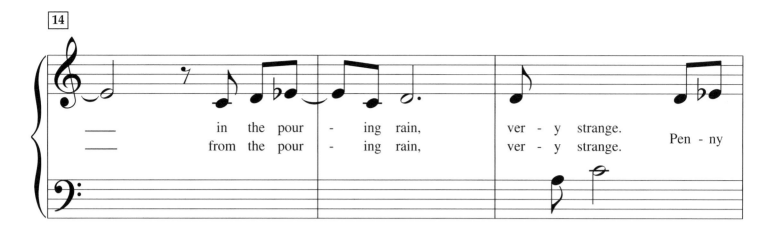

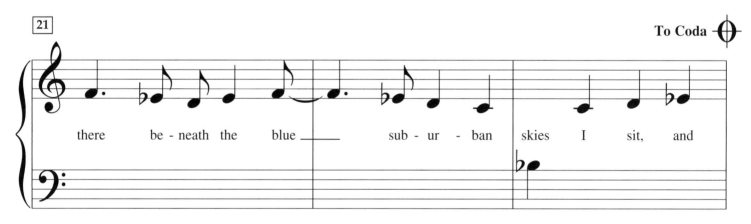

26

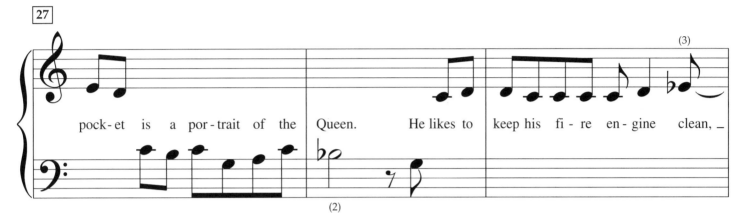

D.S. al Coda

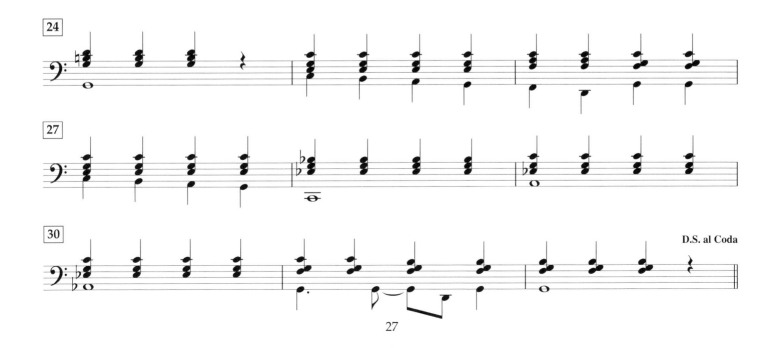

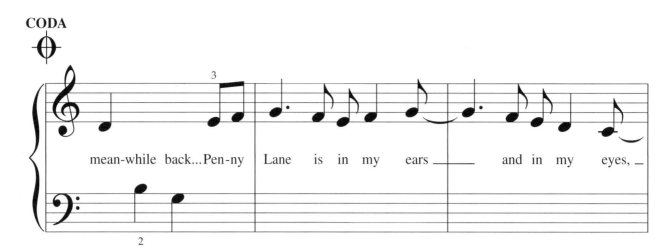

Something

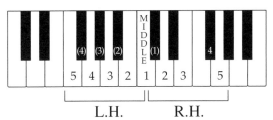

Words and Music by George Harrison

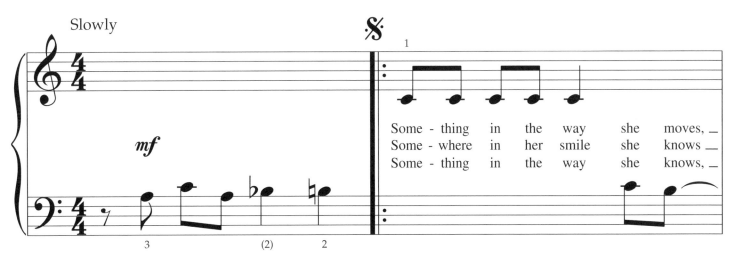

Something in the way she moves, __
Somewhere in her smile she knows, __
Something in the way she knows, __

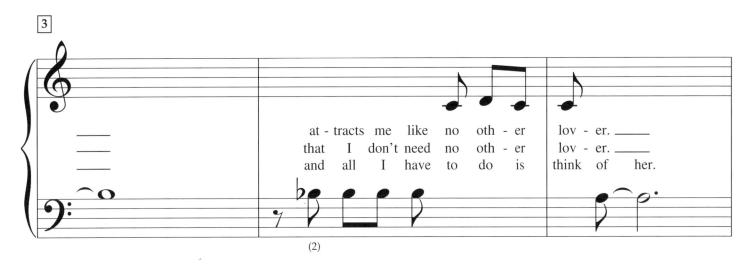

at - tracts me like no oth - er lov - er. ____
that I don't need no oth - er lov - er. ____
and all I have to do is think of her.

Duet Part (Student plays one octave higher than written.)

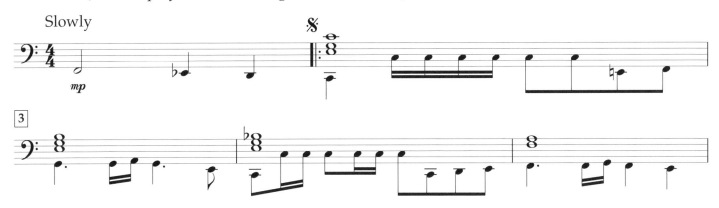

Some - thing in the way she woos ___ me. ___
Some - thing in her style that shows ___ me. ___ I
Some - thing in the things she shows ___ me. ___

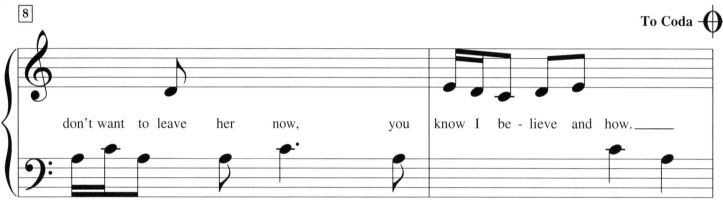

don't want to leave her now, you know I be - lieve and how. ___

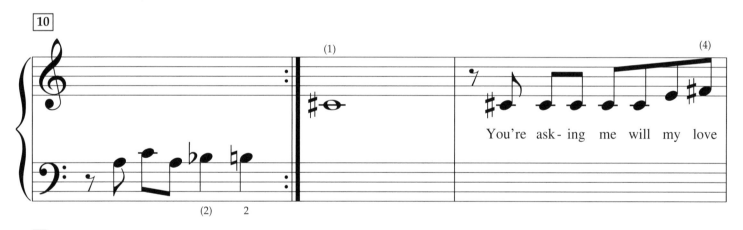

You're ask - ing me will my love

30

grow,   I   don't   know, ____   I   don't   know.

D.S. al Coda

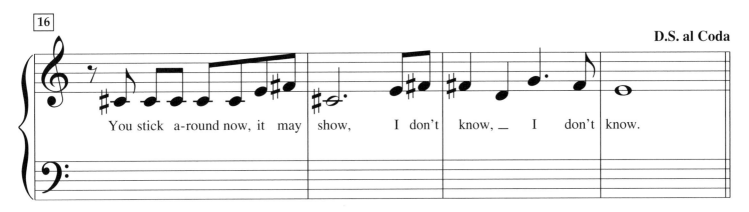

You stick a-round now, it may   show,   I   don't   know, _   I   don't   know.

CODA

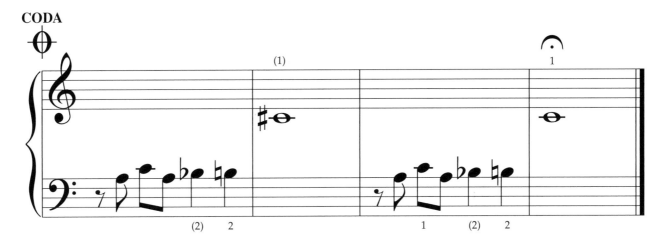

31